Incredible Invertebrates

Debra J. Housel

Consultants

Timothy Rasinski, Ph.D.
Kent State University
Bill Houska, D.V.M.
James K. Morrisey, D.V.M.

Publishing Credits

Dona Herweck Rice, *Editor-in-Chief*

Robin Erickson, *Production Director*

Lee Aucoin, *Creative Director*

Conni Medina, M.A.Ed., *Editorial Director*

Jamey Acosta, *Editor*

Heidi Kellenberger, *Editor*

Lexa Hoang, *Designer*

Lesley Palmer, *Designer*

Stephanie Reid, *Photo Editor*

Rachelle Cracchiolo, M.S.Ed., *Publisher*

Image Credits

Cover Dwight Smith/Shutterstock; p.3 Mariusz S. Jurgielewicz/Shutterstock; p.4-5 daimblond/Shutterstock; p.4 formiktopus/Shutterstock; p.5 top bottom: bmaki/Shutterstock; Levent Konuk/Shutterstock; p.6-7 ivylingpy/Shutterstock; p.6 Pavel Mikoska/Shutterstock; p.7 Oliver Hoffmann/Shutterstock; p.8-9 alslutsky/Shutterstock; p.8 Christian Ziegler/Newscom; p.9 Frederick R. McConnaughey/Photo Researchers, Inc.; p.9 inset: Dusty Cline/Shutterstock; p.10-11 Marjan Visser Photography/Shutterstock; p.10 John A. Anderson/Shutterstock; p.11 top to bottom Eye of Science/Photo Researchers, Inc.; Mark William Penny/Shutterstock; Dwight Smith/Shutterstock; p.12-13 Khoroshunova Olga/Shutterstock; p.12 Dennis Sabo/Shutterstock; p.13 top to bottom: Dudarev Mikhail/Shutterstock; JW.Alker/Photolibrary; p.14-15 mashe/Shutterstock; p.14 Kokhanchikov/Shutterstock; p.15 top to bottom: Francesc Cebria [www.ub.edu/planaria]; p.16-17 daimblond/Shutterstock; p.16 Igor Kovalchuk/Shutterstock; p.17 Bob Gibbons/Photo Researchers, Inc.; p.18-19 RAGMA IMAGES/Shutterstock; p.18 JonMilnes/Shutterstock; p.18 inset: lfstewart/Shutterstock; p.19 L. Newman & A. Flowers/Photo Researchers, Inc.; p.20-21 Mostovyi Sergii Igorevich/Shutterstock; p.20 left to right: Stuart Westmorland/Getty Images; p.21 Brian J. Skerry, George Grall/National Geographic Image Collection; p.22-23 daimblond/Shutterstock; p.22 Audrey Snider-Bell/Shutterstock; p.22 inset: Audrey Snider-Bell/Shutterstock; p.23 Rick Neese; p.24-25 NatalieJean/Shutterstock; p.24 Seow Yen Choon Kelvin/Shutterstock; p.25 Dr. Morley Read/Shutterstock; p.25 inset: Audrey Snider-Bell/Shutterstock; p.26-27 Khoroshunova Olga/Shutterstock; p.26 left to right: Yva Momatiuk & John Eastcott/Photo Researchers, Inc.; Virginia P. Weinland/Photo Researchers, Inc.; p.28 Ragma Images/Shutterstock; background: picturepartners/Shutterstock; Lukiyanova Natalia/frenta/Shutterstock

Based on writing from *TIME For Kids*.

TIME For Kids and the *TIME For Kids* logo are registered trademarks of TIME Inc. Used under license.

Teacher Created Materials

5301 Oceanus Drive
Huntington Beach, CA 92649-1030
http://www.tcmpub.com
ISBN 978-1-4333-3660-7
© 2012 Teacher Created Materials, Inc.
Printed in China
Nordica.072018.CA21800722

Table of Contents

What Is an Invertebrate?

Swish, squirm, wiggle. Creep, creep, crawl. Most animals move, but many cannot move as you do. You bend, run, hop, and climb. Some animals swish, squirm, wiggle, creep, or crawl. Others can't move at all! These animals are called **invertebrates** (in-VUR-tuh-breyts)—animals without backbones.

blue crayfish

▼ There are more than one million different invertebrates.

snail

jellyfish

Invertebrates' bodies are much simpler than yours. Instead of brains, they have a bundle of cells called a **ganglia** (GANG-glee-uh). This controls their bodies just as your brain controls yours. But since they lack brains, these animals cannot do many of the things that you can.

Invertebrates can be found in the air, under the water, and on land. Some are **carnivores** (KAHR-nuh-vohrs). They eat other animals. Ladybugs, for example, can eat 50 bugs a day!

a ladybug eating aphids

Sea anemones eat other sea animals.

Wow!

Invertebrates have rest periods, but they never fall asleep.

▼ Swarms of grasshoppers may eat every green thing for miles.

earthworm

This black-lip pearl oyster eats the dead plant and animal matter found in seawater.

Other invertebrates are **herbivores** (HUR-buh-vohrs), or plant eaters. Snails, for example, eat leaves, vegetables, and fruit.

Some invertebrates eat meat and plants. They are **omnivores** (OM-nuh-vohrs). Earthworms, for example, eat tiny pieces of rotting plants and animals found in the soil.

Simple Invertebrates

You have a heart, a stomach, and lungs. But not all animals have these organs. Sponges and coral do not.

Some invertebrates have soft bodies and a stinging body part. They use the sting for defense and to kill **prey**. If you have ever tangled with jellyfish, you know how much their stings hurt!

Sponges

Sponges live in the ocean. Until 200 years ago, people believed that sponges were plants. Now we know that they are the simplest of all **multicelled** animals.

stove-pipe sponges

Water Bear

Water bears are tiny invertebrates that live in water. They require water to obtain oxygen. They feed on plant and animal cells. Water bears are found throughout the world, including places with extreme temperatures, such as hot springs.

sea nettle

Microscopic Life

...y one-celled animals, like ...cteria, are invertebrates. But ...y are not what most people ...nk of when they hear the word ...ertebrate. They are called ...croscopic life because you ...d a microscope to see them.

Australian spotted jellyfish

Some simple invertebrates can grow new body parts! A sea star has five limbs. If one of its limbs gets torn off, a new one grows. This is called **regeneration**.

Simple invertebrates **reproduce** in odd ways. Sponges, jellyfish, and coral do so by **budding**. Young start growing on their parents' outer bodies. When a baby gets big enough, it breaks off as a separate animal.

sponges and coral

▲ If a sea star loses a leg, the leg may grow into a new sea star.

▼ underwater coral

Amazing!

If a piece of living sponge breaks off, it may grow into a new sponge. If the piece falls near the main sponge, it may also reattach.

Did you know that every earthworm is both male and female? It's true! When earthworms mate, they lay eggs inside a structure that grows around their bodies like a sleeve. The sleeve slides up over the worm's head and makes a cocoon. In a few weeks, new earthworms hatch from the cocoon.

earthworms

Most flatworms
are **parasites**. They
live on other animals'
bodies. Some
flatworms reproduce
by splitting in two.
One part has the
head. The other
has the tail. Each
piece then grows the
missing part. The
pieces become two
new flatworms.

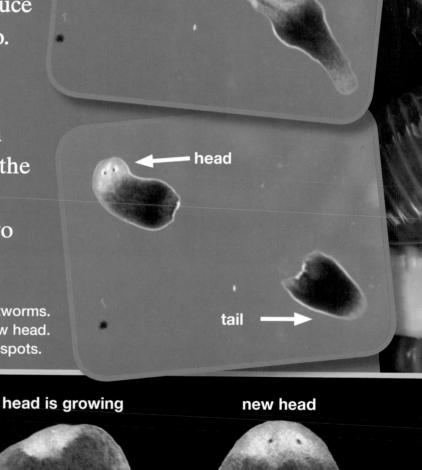

head

tail

▼ Planaria are common flatworms.
This one is growing a new head.
The two dots are its eye-spots.

tail   head is growing   new head

Mollusks

Mollusks (MOL-uhsks) have soft bodies. Most have shells covering them. Snails are mollusks with four tentacles, or feelers. The eyes at the tips of the two longest tentacles see light and dark.

▼ A snail uses its muscular foot to climb.

Aestivation

If the weather becomes hot or dry, a snail **aestivates** (ES-tuh-veyts) so that it doesn't dry out. The snail uses its foot to stick to a surface. It pulls the rest of its body into its shell. It stays like this until the weather improves.

A snail moves around using a **muscular** foot on the bottom of its body. This foot has **mucus** to help the snail glide across any surface.

Clams live most of their lives under sand or mud. They pull water through their shells. This provides them with food and oxygen. Clams are **bivalves**. That means they have two shells. Their shells are **hinged** so they can open and close them.

giant sea clam

Amazing!

Clams can live up to 400 years.

After a young clam grows a shell, it buries itself. Each year it grows larger. If you look at a clamshell, you will see lines. Just as a tree stump has rings, the clamshell's lines mark the years of its life. You can tell its age by counting the lines on its shell.

The octopus and the squid are mollusks without shells. Both live in the sea. They grab other animals with their stinging tentacles and pull them into their beaks.

These animals move by shooting jets of water from their bodies. If attacked by a **predator**, they squirt ink. The dark cloud gives the squid or octopus a chance to get away.

an octopus inking a diver

Caribbean squid

Smarty Pants!

The octopus is the smartest invertebrate and is thought to be able to think.

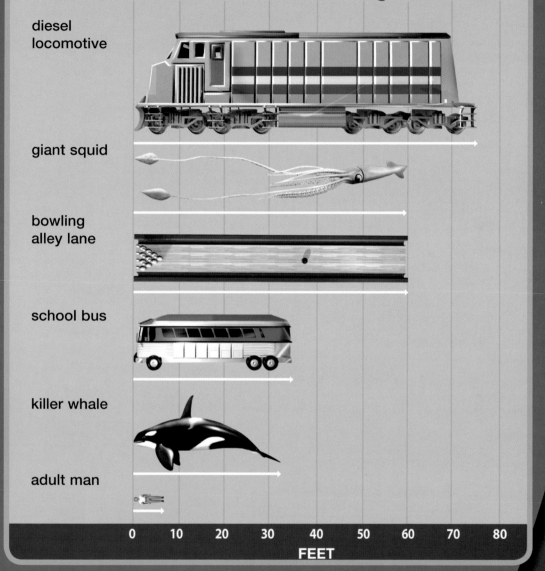

The giant squid is the largest-known invertebrate. Just look how long it can be!

diesel locomotive

giant squid

bowling alley lane

school bus

killer whale

adult man

0 10 20 30 40 50 60 70 80

FEET

Little is known about the giant squid. A live one has never been caught. Scientists study the dead squids that wash ashore. The largest ever found was 60 feet long.

Arthropods

You have leg joints. These joints let you move at the knee and the ankle. Many invertebrates have jointed legs, too. These **arthropods** (AHR-thruh-pods) include spiders, bees, lobsters, and crabs.

Most arthropods lay eggs. Some, like moths, go through stages. They change several times from birth to death.

desert hairy scorpion

Did You Know?

Insects always have six legs. Spiders are not insects because they have eight legs. This means that millipedes and centipedes are not insects, either. They may have hundreds of legs!

desert centipede

How does an arthropod's life go from beginning to end? Here is a mosquito's life from egg to adult.

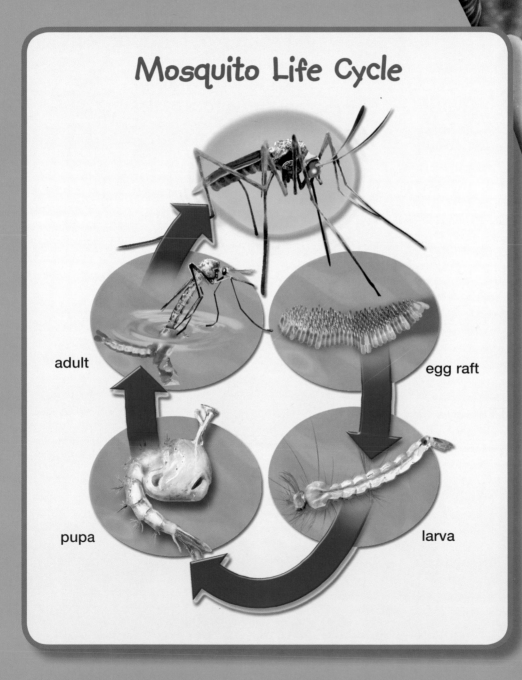

Mosquito Life Cycle

adult

egg raft

pupa

larva

You have a skeleton. It holds you up and gives you shape. Flesh covers your bones. Unlike you, arthropods have no bones. They have a hard covering on their outer bodies called an **exoskeleton**. To grow larger, an arthropod **molts**. It sheds its exoskeleton. Its body is unprotected until the new covering hardens.

Most arthropods' bodies have three **segments**. The head has eyes and a mouth. The next part is the **thorax**. The thorax often has legs and wings. The last part is the **abdomen**. This part may have more legs, a tail, or a stinger.

hermit crab

A spider wraps its prey with silk to preserve it for later.

Around the World

Insects are the only animals that live everywhere—including Antarctica!

scorpion

Spiders, scorpions, and ticks are kinds of arthropods called **arachnids**. They have eight legs and are carnivores. Spiders build webs to catch bugs. Scorpions sting their prey. Ticks can get into your pet's fur and suck its blood.

Crustaceans (kruh-STEY-shuhns) have hard outer bodies. Crabs, shrimp, lobsters, and crayfish are crustaceans. Most crabs and shrimp live in the sea, but a few can be found in freshwater. Lobsters always live in saltwater.

Crayfish look like small lobsters but live in freshwater. One kind of crayfish actually lives on land. During the day, the chimney crayfish digs a hole in a swamp. It pushes up dirt, forming a "chimney." At night, it crawls up the chimney to look for food.

Some people keep invertebrates as pets because they are quiet and don't need much care. They are also interesting to watch! It's fun to have a hermit crab, a crayfish, or an ant farm. Would you like a pet invertebrate?

crayfish chimney

red swamp crayfish

Glossary

abdomen—the back part of an arthropod

aestivates—rests during hot or dry conditions

arachnids—eight-legged arthropods that eat other animals or their blood

arthropods—invertebrates with jointed legs and a hard outer structure, like a shell (exoskeleton)

bivalves—mollusks with hinged shells

budding—reproducing by growing young on a parent's outer body

carnivores—animals that eat only meat

crustaceans—arthropods with hard outer shells and two pairs of antennae

exoskeleton—the hard outer cover of an arthropod, somewhat like a shell

ganglia—a group of nerve cells that serve as an invertebrate's simple "brain"

herbivores—animals that eat only plants

hinged—having a joint or flexible part that allows two halves to move open and closed

invertebrates—animals without backbones (spines)

microscopic life—single-celled animals that can only be seen with a microscope

mollusks—soft-bodied invertebrates that usually have shells

molts—sheds (gets rid of) the exoskeleton (the hard outer cover)

mucus—a slippery, sticky liquid-type substance that comes from living things

multicelled—having many of the tiny parts called cells that make up living things

muscular—body tissue made of muscle that enables an animal to move

omnivores—animals that eat both plants and meat

parasites—living things that live on other living things and get their nourishment from them

predator—an animal that hunts, kills, and eats other animals

prey—any animal that is hunted by another for food

regeneration—the process of regrowing a lost body part

reproduce—to create more animals like oneself

segments—the individual parts of a thing that is divided

thorax—the second of the three main parts of an arthropod

Index